USING THIS BOOK

One of the best ways of helping children learn to read is to read stories to them and with them. This way they learn what **reading** *is, and they will* gradually come to recognize many words and begin to read for themselves.

First, read the story on the left-hand pages aloud to the child.

Reread the story as often as the child enjoys hearing it. Talk about the pictures as you go.

Later the child will be able to read the words under the pictures on the right-hand pages.

The pages at the back of the book will give you some ideas for helping your child to read.

© Text and layout SHEILA McCULLAGH MCMLXXXV
© In publication LADYBIRD BOOKS LTD MCMLXXXV
Loughborough, England
LADYBIRD BOOKS, INC.
Lewiston, Maine 04240 U.S.A.

Printed in England

The Magic Box

written by SHEILA McCULLAGH
illustrated by GAVIN ROWE

This book belongs to:

Ladybird Books

Sarah and Davy
lived in Puddle Lane.
There was a big, old house
at the end of the lane,
with a big garden.
Most of the house was empty,
but a magician lived in the attic.
He liked children, and
he didn't mind a bit
if they played in his garden.

the Magician's garden

One day, Sarah was outside
in Puddle Lane.
She had a wooden cart.
One of the wheels had fallen off.
Sarah was just putting the wheel
back on again
when she looked up, and
saw Mrs. Pitter-Patter.

Sarah looked up, and
saw Mrs. Pitter-Patter.

Mrs. Pitter-Patter lived in Puddle Lane,
and she was always asking questions.
"Sarah!" cried Mrs. Pitter-Patter.
"Whatever are you doing?
You'll make your dress all dirty,
and your mother will be
very angry with you!"

"No, she won't, Mrs. Pitter-Patter,"
said Sarah. "I've got my old clothes on.
It's my birthday, and the Magician
said that he would leave a present
in the garden for me.
He said it was a big one,
so I'm taking my cart,
to carry it home."

Sarah and
Mrs. Pitter-Patter

"You'll tear your clothes on the bushes,"
cried Mrs. Pitter-Patter.
"Surely your mother doesn't let you
play in the Magician's garden!"

"Yes, she does," said Sarah.
"She knows the Magician.
He's a friend of ours.
It's a lovely place to play."

Davy came along the lane.
He had a rope in his hand.

Davy had a rope.

There were two big knobs
at one end of the cart.
Davy and Sarah tied the ends
of the rope to the knobs.

"That's the wrong way to tie it,"
said Mrs. Pitter-Patter.

"We always tie it this way,
Mrs. Pitter-Patter," said Davy.

Mrs. Pitter-Patter shook her head,
and went back down Puddle Lane,
muttering to herself.

Mrs. Pitter-Patter
went back down
Puddle Lane.

Davy pushed the garden gates open,
and Sarah pulled the cart through.
The rope worked very well.
Davy shut the gates, and
Sarah looked all around, to see
if she could see her birthday present.

Sarah and Davy
went into the garden.

She saw a big box
by the hollow tree.
"There it is! Look!" she cried.
She ran over to the tree.
The box was wrapped in red paper,
and tied with a golden ribbon.
A big white card
was propped up against it.
Sarah's name was written on the card
in big letters.

Sarah saw a big box.

"What is it?" asked Davy,
running across to the tree.

"How do I know, till I've opened it?"
said Sarah. "I'll open it now."

She took off the ribbon, and
pulled off the paper, and
uncovered a beautiful box.

The box was painted blue and gold,
and there was a big red button
on the top.

Sarah and the box

"I wonder what's inside,"
said Sarah, looking at the box.
"How do you open it?"

"Wait a minute," said Davy.
"There's something written on the back
of the card. Look! It says,
    'Don't open the box.
    Push the red button.'"

"What good is a box,
if you can't open it?" asked Sarah.

"It might be a magic box,"
said Davy. "You'd better do
what the Magician says."

"All right," said Sarah. "I'll try it."
She pushed the red button.

Sarah pushed
the red button.

At once, the box began to play a tune.
Sarah felt her feet begin to dance.
She couldn't stop them.
The tune was a dancing tune,
and her feet danced with it.

Davy was dancing, too.
He couldn't help it.
They joined hands, and
danced around and around,
until the music stopped.

Sarah and Davy
began to dance.

"It's a music box!" cried Sarah.
(She was out of breath.)
"What a lovely present!"

"It's a **magic** music box," said Davy.
"I couldn't stop dancing."

"Neither could I," said Sarah.
"My feet wouldn't stop.
Let's take the box back to Puddle Lane."

They lifted the box into the cart,
and pulled it back carefully
to the garden gates.

Sarah and Davy
went back to
Puddle Lane.

When they got to Puddle Lane,
they saw Mr. Gotobed.
Mr. Gotobed lived in the house
next to the Magician's garden.
He spent most of the day in bed,
sleeping. But sometimes he took
his chair outside into the lane,
and went to sleep in the sunshine.
He was fast asleep now,
sitting in his chair.

Sarah and Davy
saw Mr. Gotobed.

Sarah looked at Davy.
"I'm going to push the button,
and see what happens!"
she whispered.

She pushed the red button.
The music box began to play.

Sarah pushed
the red button.

Old Mr. Gotobed woke up with a start.
He jumped out of his chair,
and began to dance.
Sarah and Davy joined hands, and
danced around until the music stopped.

"Well!" cried Mr. Gotobed, as he sat down
in his chair again. "Well, well, well!
I haven't danced like that
since I was a boy.
That's a wonderful music box, Sarah!"

"It was a birthday present, from
the Magician," said Sarah.

"A present from the Magician!"
said Mr. Gotobed. "That explains it.
It's a **magic** music box."

Mr. Gotobed
began to dance.

Mrs. Pitter-Patter came pattering
up the lane. She saw the box.
"What have you got there, Sarah?"
she cried.

"It's my birthday present
from the Magician," said Sarah.

"Nonsense!" cried Mrs. Pitter-Patter.
"The Magician would never give you
a beautiful box like that!
You must put it back
where you found it.
And what's that button?"

"Don't touch it, Mrs. Pitter-Patter!"
cried Davy.

Mrs. Pitter-Patter
saw the box.

"Of course I'll touch it,
if I want to," said Mrs. Pitter-Patter.
And she pressed the red button.
This time, the box didn't play
its dancing tune. It began to sing:

"Mrs. Pitter-Patter
patters up the lane.
Mrs. Pitter-Patter
patters home again.
Mrs. Pitter-Patter
telling people what to do,
pitter-patter, clitter-clatter,
chitter-chatter-choo!"

The box began to sing.

As soon as the box began to sing,
Mrs. Pitter-Patter's feet began to dance.
She twirled around and around
in the lane.
"Oh!" cried Mrs. Pitter-Patter. "Oh!
Whatever is it?
Whatever is happening to me?"

Mrs. Pitter-Patter
began to dance.

Mrs. Pitter-Patter was the only one
who danced to **that** tune.
Sarah and Davy and Mr. Gotobed
stood watching her dance, until
at last the box stopped singing,
and Mrs. Pitter-Patter went in
the door of her own house.

Mrs. Pitter-Patter
danced down
Puddle Lane.

"I hope she's all right," said Davy.
"She was dancing very fast."

"Oh, she'll be all right," said Mr. Gotobed.
"It's very happy music.
I don't think it could hurt her.
I enjoyed my dance.
But you'd better take that box
home with you now, Sarah.
I'm worn out, and I'm going
to take a little nap."

Mr. Gotobed sat down in his chair.
He put his handkerchief over his head,
and went back to sleep.

Mr. Gotobed
went back to sleep.

"It's a wonderful present,"
said Davy, looking at the box.

"Yes, it is," said Sarah.
"Let's take it home,
and show it to everyone."

So Sarah and Davy took
the magic music box home.

Sarah and Davy
took the box home.

Notes for the parent/teacher

Turn back to the beginning, and print the child's name in the space on the title page, using ordinary, not capital letters.

Now go through the book again. Look at each picture and talk about it. Point to the caption below, and read it aloud yourself.

Run your finger under the words as you read, so that the child learns that reading goes from left to right.

Encourage the child to read the words under the illustrations. Don't rush in with the word before he/she has had time to think, but don't leave him/her struggling.

Read this story as often as the child likes hearing it. The more opportunities he/she has to look at the illustrations and **read** the captions with you, the more he/she will come to recognize the words.

If you have several books, let the child choose which story he/she would like.

Mr. Gotobed woke up.